The Authentic
Confidence
Handbook

A Mindset Manual for Professional
Women of Color!

Hayley Dennis

Dedication

For my amazing parents who inspired me to be myself and to do anything, I wanted without limits! And, to my always supportive husband, Jovon, and my sisters Beth and Robin.

Table Of
Contents

HOW TO USE THIS
Guidebook!

My hope is that what I have learned will help you navigate your corporate journey.

Each chapter covers an issue many women of color have encountered throughout their corporate careers that can and will chip away at your confidence over time and affect how you see yourself. Each of the Ten Tips for Building Authentic Confidence is divided into an introduction to the issue, the solution, and the **P.T.A. (Pause, Think, and Ask)** section which is for immediate, in-the-moment help with the problem - your emergency toolbox where you can turn to for immediate assistance and guidance.

Intro-
duction.

Many books and articles have been written about building and maintaining confidence. I have read many of these publications throughout my corporate career.

However, something was lacking. There was a disconnect between what I was reading and what I was experiencing. One day after I finished reading a book on confidence, I walked to my kitchen to get a snack and as I passed a wall mirror, I paused to look at myself. That's when it hit me! I was reading and devouring material to help me navigate the corporate world and build confidence, but - the information was not geared toward me - an African American woman. I pride myself on being able to read and take in information from many sources and make it apply to my circumstances, but this felt different.

This caused me to dive a little deeper and discover how I can be my genuine authentic self.

Throughout my corporate career, I have found myself surrounded by people who don't look like me.

Although we may have travelled the same career path and obtained the same education, their experiences were different from mine. I often found myself showing up every day feeling like I had to prove myself. I had to be smarter, wittier, and more poised than my coworkers.

Systemic racism has always been present in the workplace and still exists today. This has made people of color (POC) feel they have to work harder than their white peers. There are countless biases that are encountered before we even step foot into the office. Our name and appearance can automatically put us at a disadvantage, and that's just during the hiring process. In some circumstances, I had more experience, more knowledge, more education, and more dedication...yet I was still judged differently.

This took a toll on my confidence.

I eventually found myself speaking up less, taking less initiative, and shrinking into the shadows. Of course, I was still producing stellar work because I had been taught to always do my best, but now I was keeping my head down and performing quietly.

My confidence waned and imposter syndrome was settling in; how did I get here?

I started working in the corporate world at the age of 16. I began an apprenticeship in Finance in my junior year of high school. I remained with the company as an intern throughout college. Those seven years introduced me to a world I knew absolutely nothing about, but truly set me up for success.

As I look back over the last 20 years, did I exhibit the most confidence that I could have? Did I show up as my authentic self in every situation? Did I have mentors that looked like me providing guidance during my corporate journey? Did I even know what it meant to show up as my genuine self?

Of course, the answer is "No." I wish I had known in my 20s the things I know now, but my experiences have helped me become the woman I am today.

HERE ARE MY

Top 10 Tips for Building Authentic Confidence!

Tip. 1 Stop Being The Fixer.

Take a minute and think about your daily attire, is there a cape with a "S" on it?

What does the "S" stand for, you may be wondering?

Let me tell you: *Superwoman.*

Yes, as women we are taught to be the Superwoman. Save the situation, find a solution, and make it work - sometimes at all costs. This can be applicable when it comes to our family and our own personal wants and desires, but are we required to be the Superwoman at work?

You are more capable, but does that require you to always be the solution to every problem? Do you find yourself getting the projects that no one wants or the problem projects with the difficult stakeholders?

Oftentimes your leaders may tell you that you are amazing and that you are doing a wonderful job. The reason you are getting these projects is because you are the most capable person on the team and you are their top performer.

Let me introduce you to gaslighting! Gaslighting is a form of bullying in the workplace and can ultimately cause you to question your sanity, validity and worth. You begin to believe what your leaders or coworkers are telling you and you find yourself second-guessing everything you do or believing that you are the solution to everything. Are you getting paid top performer salary? Are you working late hours after everyone else has left the office or shut down their laptop for the day? Have you found yourself solving problems and producing solutions only to have someone else take credit for your work?

If you answered "yes" to any of these questions, you have become the Fixer.

There are many reasons that we find ourselves in these situations. For example, if you are a team leader, you don't want your team to be looked upon as a failure. So, what do you do?

You overcompensate for the team. You fix their mistakes, or worse, you do their work for them instead of using those situations as teaching opportunities.

Here's another scenario. Other leaders in the company come to you for assistance on projects that really should be handled by other teams. You may be an individual contributor and your leader is constantly tapping you to help other teammates complete their tasks, or giving you projects that are outside of your job duties.

Women of color constantly feel the need to prove themselves in the corporate world, and this contributes to the fixer mindset.

Your worth and confidence are then tied into feeling needed.

To be clear, I'm not saying don't be a team player, but has the "ask" become the norm rather than an occasional request? Look at your projects over the past few months; see any patterns?

How To Do It?

To combat the Fixer, don't be afraid to say NO! This may mean that your team misses a deadline or isn't able to take on an extra project.

Set boundaries and priorities and stick to them.

If someone asks you to help and your plate is full, let them know that. Perhaps share your current priorities and offer to move some things around if their request has higher priority.

Don't be afraid to ask for help! This is not a weakness. Getting assistance and completing something on time is a confidence booster and builds relationships.

It may be tempting to roll up your sleeves and get in the weeds with the team, and there will be occasions when this will need to happen. However, allowing the team to learn, to make mistakes, and to figure out solutions on their own will enhance their professional development and sharpen their problem-solving skills.

They will thank you later! This new mindset of saying "no" when others come to you for help might be a difficult adjustment at first, but the more you stick to your boundaries, the others will too. You can complete your duties and feel confident knowing that you did a good job and put your needs ahead of others. This will give you time to focus on your own professional development and your own strategic planning. Also, you will have time to focus on self-care; specifically, your own mental and emotional well-being.

PAUSE, THINK &
ASK: (P.T.A.)

The next time someone approaches you with a Fixer request, **Pause, Think, and Ask Yourself:**

☐ Is this serving my end goal or someone else's goal?

☐ What would I be sacrificing to assist this person?

If the answers to those questions make you feel confident and secure, then proceed. If they don't, keep it moving!

Pause.

Think...

Ask!

(TAKE SOME TIME AND REFLECT)

"One of the lessons that I grew up with was to always stay true to yourself, and never let what somebody else says distract you from your goals."

– MICHELLE OBAMA

Tip. 2 Stop Being The Perfecti-onist!

As young girls, many of you were taught that you must be the best and you have to always give your all in everything that you do, failure was not an option. Conversely, some of you were told you would never succeed, so you set for yourself an unrealistic goal of perfectionism.

Being a brown girl, I knew I would have to work harder and that when people looked at me, they would often form a biased opinion. For many, this too fuels a constant quest for perfection.

I remember when I got laid off for the first time and I was still living at home. At the end of the first week and collecting unemployment, my Dad asked me, "Did you find a job yet? No one is going to be laying around here." Although I explained to him that I had six weeks of unemployment, I immediately began looking for a job which I found a week later. I did not want him to view me as lazy and not measure up to his standard of what I should be doing, I needed to be perfect and find a job ASAP.

Reflecting on that time, I wished I had taken that break. How often do we get paid breaks in our corporate career? On the other hand, I might have missed the job that allowed me to work with an amazing group of women that looked like me and to have my first and only African American woman manager. She was fire! She was the epitome of confidence. While she always strived to give her best and continually work on her professional growth, she knew where to put her energy and realized that pleasing others was not her main priority. She showed up as her authentic confident self and made no apologies!

THESE FOUR WORDS CAN PUT AN EXTREMELY HEAVY WEIGHT ON YOU.

Judgment, Expectation, Fear, Failure (JEFF)

Judgment

from others (even those we love) can throw you into a spiral. Constantly trying to measure up to what you think others want from you can be exhausting and a major confidence drainer. What if they don't like it? What if they find an error? What if I should have included more? Are you guilty of the "what ifs"?

Expectations

are wonderful and help you achieve your goals, but do you find yourself **ALWAYS** setting higher expectations for yourself than required? Take a moment and ponder that question. Am I setting these higher expectations to benefit myself or am I doing it to be viewed as perfect in the eyes of my manager and/or team? Set expectations that make sense for your personal circumstances and that build your confidence up, not tear it down.

Fear,

particularly the fear of # Failure,

is a beast...a sly and ferocious beast that works quietly to sabotage your confidence. No one wakes up and says I want to be a failure today. But we are imperfect, and we will sometimes fail. I have learned that instead of viewing failures as something negative, to view them as opportunities to learn and improve. What can I do better next time? What did this failure teach me about myself? Changing our mindset around failure and reframing it into a learning experience can help increase our confidence so that the next time we experience that situation or something similar, we are confident about how to proceed toward a more positive outcome.

You can allow perfectionism to cause you to sacrifice your time and energy on things that don't deserve it.

How To Do It?

When approaching a task/project, decide what outcome would make you feel most confident and then proceed. You can make changes along the way, but make sure those changes are what you want and not to please others. People pleasing can throw you into a never-ending spiral and make you feel like it will never be good enough and thus you will never complete what you are working on.

Set realistic goals that you can achieve. Oftentimes, you may find yourself creating big goals and then experiencing disappointment when you do not accomplish them.

Start by breaking down large goals into smaller bite-size goals. Completing each small goal will push you toward achieving the large goal.

Fall in love with yourself...yes...love every single piece of you! Appreciating who you are and what your strengths are will enable you to find enjoyment, contentment and happiness in your capabilities, and not in comparison to others. Nobody is perfect and you should stop putting pressure on yourself to be perfect, and embrace your imperfections, they are yours and make you the unique individual you are.

Perfect is great, done is even better!
Break up with JEFF!

PAUSE, THINK &
ASK: (P.T.A.)

The next time you feel perfectionism creeping up on you, **Pause, Think, and Ask Yourself:**

☐ Am I striving after my definition of complete and done, or someone else's?

☐ What would I be sacrificing to achieve perfectionism?

If the answers to those questions make you feel confident and secure, then proceed. If they don't, get rid of what is driving you to feel like you have to be a perfectionist!

Pause.

Think...

Ask!

(TAKE SOME TIME AND REFLECT)

"Done is better than perfect."

– SHERYL SANDBERG

Clear
Tip. 3 Out
Imposter
Syndrome

Imposter syndrome has become a very popular topic in the last few years and constantly comes up in discussions with my clients. When I think about imposter syndrome, it really encompasses doubting your abilities and feeling like a fraud. You may find yourself questioning whether you're deserving of your accomplishments. You were only successful because of special circumstances, not because of your talent, qualifications, or experience. At some point in our careers, we will all experience this syndrome in some form. The key is to not remain in this mindset.

Some symptoms of imposter syndrome include self-doubts, low self-confidence, berating yourself, fear of failure, sabotaging your own success, feeling like you don't belong, and the list can go on.

Allowing imposter syndrome to take root in your mind can cause your confidence to drop significantly.

The result: you begin to second guess and over-think every decision you make. Like some health conditions, imposter syndrome can obscure the real cause of your feelings. Identify the true blocker of your confidence. Here are some ways to do that.

How To Do It?

First, internalize and own your success! When you focus on your strengths, you remind yourself what you excel at and what makes you unique, not in comparison to anyone else.

Second, learn to take your mistakes and failures in stride, growing from them rather than harboring on what you did wrong. Something that has really helped me combat failures is developing a healthy response when I fail. View them as personal growth opportunities, occasions to reflect on how

how you can continue to better yourself. Give yourself the space and grace to think about it and reframe it into something neutral or positive.

Third, visualize success. Make a specific plan of what success looks like for you. Defining your personal success path allows you to build upon what makes you exceptional. I cannot stress the importance of visualization. When we see ourselves living and thriving in a successful environment, we increase our belief in ourselves and what we are capable of, and our confidence grows.

When was the last time you celebrated a success? We often celebrate our big wins, but what about small accomplishments? Celebrate those too, they deserve recognition. Celebrating your wins, no matter how big or small, will remind you of what you've accomplished and can shift your focus to continue thinking about how to grow and continue to be successful. Focus on giving your best and not being the best!

One way to constantly remind yourself of your accomplishments is to create a brag book. You can do this with paper or create an electronic document. Capture all your accomplishments as far back as you can remember and continue to add to the list.

When you feel imposter syndrome creeping in, get out your brag book and remind yourself of the wonderful things you have done.

When you find yourselves in a new role or taking on a new challenge, be vulnerable. This takes courage. Remember, vulnerability can help you to really see yourself and move forward with confidence.

PAUSE, THINK & ASK: (P.T.A.)

The next time you feel imposter syndrome in a situation, **Pause, Think, and Ask Yourself:**

☐   Am I truly being an imposter or is this who I am?

☐   What did I do to get here (was it my own hard work)?

If the answers to those questions make you feel confident and secure, then proceed. If they don't, re-examine the situation and identify areas of change/improvement that will allow you to feel confident and kick imposter syndrome to the curb!

Pause.

Think...

Ask!

(TAKE SOME TIME AND REFLECT)

"There's no more powerful lesson than knowing that your setbacks will one day help you succeed."

– RESHMA SAUJANI

Create *Tip. 4*
Bound-
aries.

How far are you willing to go to prove to someone else that you deserve to be there? What will it cost you? Will it cost you time, family, friends, dignity, and self-worth?

Let's reframe that question: How far are you willing to go to prove to yourself that you deserve to be there? Don't let anyone make you feel like you are not good enough. Take a moment and reflect.

How many times did you push yourself past the limit to prove that you were good enough? You stayed late working on a project and missed your child's performance only to have someone else take credit or not even have your work used. You started early and stayed late all week to complete a big task, only to not be recognized as a contributor.

Unfortunately, these microaggressions have become common in the workplace and yet, you are expected to come in each day with a smile on your face. If you display any sign of weakness or fragility, you are called emotional. If you respond back or give pushback, you are labelled the

The ABW (*Angry Black Woman*)

The ultimate microaggression that can be used to diminish your worth.

This All Stops Now!

How To Do It?

From this day forward, set boundaries and decide what serves you and your purpose and what does not. It is not always easy to set boundaries, but the results and benefits of setting boundaries are tremendous. There are quite a few ways to begin the process, try some of these steps and see what works for you. Make a list of what is important to you. Note why it is important to you, and if you did not have this in your life, would it matter?

Consider your current goals and if you have not been able to spend time accomplishing them. What barriers are standing in your way? If work is preventing you from accomplishing your goals or if work is getting in the way of the things that are most important to you in life, it's time to set some boundaries.

Stick to the hours that you set for your workday. Granted, things can slip in at times that can cause you to have long days or emergencies, but is that the norm? If your workday ends at 5:30 pm and an email notification pops up on your phone at 5:50 pm, are you going to read the message and respond? If you receive an instant message from a co-worker at 6:15 pm asking if they can call you with a quick question, are you going to take the call? Will the Fixer or Perfectionist appear or will you enforce the boundaries you have created?

Block out time on your calendar to protect your mental and emotional well-being. Even if people ignore your blocks and schedule over your time, respect yourself enough to decline their request and reschedule at a time that you have available.

There is another aspect to setting boundaries that you may find yourself battling. You have no problem setting boundaries, but you find yourself constantly explaining yourself and your actions.

You need to leave on time to go to an exercise class or get dinner started for your family.

Or, perhaps, your manager calls your name just as you shut down your laptop. You immediately begin explaining why you need to leave right now, but 15 minutes later your laptop is open and you're helping your coworker or sitting in your manager's office. Let's rewind and try this again. It's the end of the day and you shut down your laptop and you hear your name as you head to the door. Your response:

"I'm headed out, send me an email, or grab some time on my calendar tomorrow and we can discuss. Have an enjoyable evening!"

You didn't over-explain or make an excuse for protecting your time and sticking to your boundaries. The more you begin to do this, the more it will come naturally. You will feel more confident making time and space for what is important to you and others will respect your boundaries.

PAUSE, THINK &
ASK: (P.T.A.)

The next time you feel your boundaries are being crossed, **Pause, Think, and Ask Yourself:**

☐ What does it look like if I allow this boundary to be crossed?

☐ What does it look like if I enforced my boundaries?

☐ Who benefits and who suffers if I allow my boundaries to continually be crossed?

If the answers to those questions make you feel confident and secure, then proceed. If they don't, immediately consider what you can do to put your boundaries back in place!

Pause.

Think...

Ask!

(TAKE SOME TIME AND REFLECT)

"Deal with yourself as an individual worthy of respect, and make everyone else deal with you the same way."

– NIKKI GIOVANNI

Identify
Tip. 5 *Your*
Strengths!

When was the last time you sat down and thought about your strengths? Usually, this question comes up when we're interviewing for a new position but take some time right now and reflect on your strengths. It is important to reflect on and identify your strengths. Knowing your strengths allows you to operate in your center of excellence and influence. Have you ever met someone who was considered a thought leader in their field of study or industry? You never doubt what they say and you may even hang onto their every word. Why?

Because you view them as an expert in their field and you trust what they are saying.

Can this be true of you?

Tapping into your strengths enables you to feel confident to speak and act in an authoritative way and exhibit executive presence whenever you step into a room.

Drawing upon your strengths helps you to combat your insecurities and push self-doubt aside so that you can operate in your area of expertise. The more that you tap into your strengths the more your imposter syndrome will shrink and your self-confidence will increase.

How To Do It?

Grab a notebook, phone or laptop and start jotting down every single one of your strengths. Small or large, they make you who you are. Go back as far as you can remember. When you focus and think about your strengths it reinforces positive thoughts in your mind. Your strengths are what guided you along your career journey. This is an exercise that I have my coaching clients go through because it helps them recall abilities and talents they may have forgotten. Remembering what got you where you are helps you to continue to grow and increase your confidence along the way.

After working in a corporate environment for some time, you may begin to feel stagnant. If you are not learning new things or receiving praise and recognition, your confidence can start to diminish. You may begin to think you are unworthy and start doubting your own abilities. If you are given difficult projects and difficult people to manage, do not despair. Don't let it break you. The next steps you take are crucial to building your confidence and placing yourself in an environment where you can continue to grow.

Grab your brag book that you created earlier, review your accomplishments, and connect your strengths to each accomplishment. Recognize the strong, talented, capable woman that did these amazing things and think about how your strengths can take you to the next place you want to be.

Whatever it may be, make sure it is something you want and not what someone else thinks you should do. There have been occasions, throughout my career, when I was told by my leaders what they thought would be a good fit for me. Sometimes the advice made sense and was beneficial. Other times, it was the typical path for a woman of color, lower paying, less visible positions. I wasn't encouraged to pursue leadership or higher visibility roles, despite being highly qualified.

Recognizing your strengths will allow you to step into new territories and explore new possibilities! Don't underestimate your strengths and what got you where you are today. If you are content in your current role and where you are in your career, own it! Just make sure that it's what you want, and that you are not letting other people's opinions and thoughts keep you in a place you don't want to be.

Your job does not define who you are, YOU define who you are!

PAUSE, THINK &
ASK: (P.T.A.)

The next time you find yourself feeling insecure,
Pause, Think, and Ask Yourself:

☐   If I removed this insecurity, which one of my strengths could I replace it with to have a favorable outcome?

☐   What hidden strengths can I uncover to assist me in showing up more confidently today?

If the answers to those questions make you feel confident and secure, then proceed. If they don't, begin highlighting your strengths and looking for daily opportunities to tap into your strengths so that you are able to showcase them effortlessly!

Pause.

Think...

Ask!

(TAKE SOME TIME AND REFLECT)

"You've gotta do things that make you happy. As women, we tend to give away a lot.

We take care of a lot of people, and we can't forget to take care of ourselves."

– JENNIFER LOPEZ

Find Your
Tip. 6 *Voice!*

Remember your elementary school days? Do you recall a time when you maybe stood up to a bully or told off the girl on the playground that was constantly bothering you or always had something smart to say to you? You may have thought long and hard about what you wanted to say and then practiced it in the mirror before going to school.

How did you feel after you used your voice to express yourself? I hope you felt like you were on top of the world. Now think about the last time you used your voice and had that same feeling in the workplace. In the corporate world, a woman with a voice is usually called loud, emotional, opinionated and/or headstrong.

To avoid these labels, we start to silence our voices. We speak up less in meetings, we don't share our ideas or solutions, we let people say things that probably should be addressed and eventually find ourselves sitting in meetings with the infamous resting bitch face. If we do speak, the perception of our tone becomes the focus and not what we said.

Or, after speaking, someone begins explaining what they think we were trying to say.

Cue the ABW.

One day I was sitting in a meeting with a vendor and four other male colleagues. I was the only woman and the only person of color. We were discussing an issue and troubleshooting to find a solution. I had an idea, but I hesitated. After a few minutes of an internal pep talk, I shared my idea. One colleague responded with a chuckle and said I didn't know what I was talking about. I was fuming inside!

Although I could have handled this situation in many different ways, instead I remained quiet. After about 30 minutes, the vendor suggested we try my idea and it worked. I then spoke and said, "I guess I did know what I was talking about!" That experience helped me to find my voice and never again be afraid to speak up and share my ideas and thoughts. I also learned that every situation does not deserve a response or a reaction.

Sometimes people will try and bait you and set up a situation to awaken the ABW.

However, don't allow anyone to silence your voice.

ALWAYS SEEK TO MAINTAIN A CALM, NON-ARGUMENTATIVE TONE.

The eye rolls or heavy sighs we may experience from others while we are speaking can be a motivator to speak up even more often.

Decide when and where you want to share your thoughts. Your ideas matter and can bring a new outlook and fresh perspective. Also, you never know who you may be encouraging. I have observed women leaders speak up in meetings and hold their ground while remaining professional and polished and this inspired me to want to imitate their example.

How To Do It?

Each morning, think about how you can use your voice to empower yourself or someone else. It may be a simple "hello" or acknowledging a job well done, don't hold back from using your voice.

Your ideas and thoughts are just as important as the next person's. In your next meeting, identify some areas ahead of time where you can make a contribution to the discussion.

You may be sitting on an idea and have failed to share it, this is your opportunity to let your voice be heard, and share that idea at the next appropriate time.

Even if it is glossed over or not acknowledged, celebrate the fact that you spoke up and took the opportunity to share your knowledge and thoughts.

Do you have topics or subjects that you enjoy having conversations about? Or there may be interests and topics that you want to learn more about. Start now! Choose one topic that you would like to learn more about and increase your knowledge in that area and then share what you are learning with another person.

This will allow you to feel more comfortable sharing your thoughts with others in groups or in 1:1 conversations. The more you practice this, the more you will find yourself speaking up and getting involved in conversations without thinking about what others think.

PAUSE, THINK & ASK: (P.T.A.)

The next time you feel like you are not being heard, **Pause, Think, and Ask Yourself:**

☐ If I remain silent, who wins?

☐ How could I possibly change my approach to ensure that I am being heard?

If the answers to those questions make you feel confident and secure, then proceed. If they don't, decide if you need to be heard in this specific situation or can you wait until the next opportunity, after all, it is their loss!

Pause.

Think...

Ask!

(TAKE SOME TIME AND REFLECT)

"Each time a woman stands up for herself without knowing it, possibly without claiming it, she stands up for all women."

– MAYA ANGELOU

Define
Tip. 7 *Your*
Success.

How do you measure your personal success? Is it based on what someone else has defined for you as success? When we are children, it's our parents and teachers who set the bar for success for us.

As we got older, we were influenced by a broader community that may have included our parents, professors, peers, and leaders we admired. After entering the workforce, our managers set the standards of success. We were continually striving after the success that was outlined for us.

Now, as an adult, it's time to define what success means and looks like for YOU! Success for a woman of color in the corporate world is challenging.

When we enter that environment we must deal with the biases and perceptions that immediately arise when they see the color of our skin. These realities could negatively affect how we view ourselves. My parents instilled in me, at an early age, that I was beautiful, smart, and intelligent.

I could be anything I wanted, and nobody should tell me otherwise. I am so thankful for this mindset because it has remained in me until this day. It's helped me to keep going when I was passed over for a promotion, didn't get the promised pay raise, or despite my brand new, out-of-the-box ideas, I would not be getting a high rating on my performance review.

These experiences taught me that I was striving to prove to others that I deserved to be there, but I was losing myself and my voice. I didn't know what to do except keep going and doing what was outlined as a success for me. I was

in the game, but I was not playing my game. I was playing their game.

What is the game? The corporate world for many individuals is about climbing the corporate ladder and increasing their salary and impact. For POC, many times we are not afforded these opportunities for growth and advancement. So you begin to adapt yourself to fit the mold of what you think will get you a seat at the table and further your career.

Your definition and path to success get sidetracked or derailed. Then you must ask yourself:

Am I striving to fulfill my vision or am I playing their game (their definition of success) and fulfilling their vision?

When you stop and reflect and decide that it's about time to start playing the game your way, then you can create and define your success.

Think of it this way: You are behind the wheel steering, directing, and driving to your destination. You define the stops along the journey. You call the shots and make the decisions that will bring you satisfaction and make you feel like a whole person.

Stepping into your defined success can be the best confidence booster. Mapping out your success map ensures that you show up as your authentic self.

How To Do It?

Take a moment right now and think about what success looks like for you. Write it down and then map out your journey to get there. You may be living in it already; if you are, that is awesome!

Keep going and don't let any interference cause you to get off track. If this is new for you and you realize that you have been going after someone else's vision of success for you, this is your time to define your success. Be selfish, put yourself first.

No matter how small or how big, write it down. Create a vision board. Visualizing your success makes it real, not just a dream. Then think about how you will achieve this success. Build it out into small doable steps and watch how your vision becomes a reality. Enlist the help of those who you trust and who support you. As you complete each small goal, do something to celebrate! Each small success builds confidence to get to the ultimate success. There will be setbacks and bumps in the road, maybe even some potholes, but don't give up.

PAUSE, THINK &
ASK: (P.T.A.)

The next time you feel like you are living someone else's vision of success, **Pause, Think, and Ask Yourself:**

☐ How did I get to the point of striving after someone else's vision and not my own?

☐ Have I clearly defined my personal vision of success for my life?

If the answers to those questions make you feel confident and secure, then proceed. If they don't, get started right away designing your vision of success!

Pause.

Think...

Ask!

"Greatness is not measured by what a man or woman accomplishes, but by the opposition he or she has overcome to reach his goals."

– DOROTHY HEIGHT

Change
Tip. 8 Your
Mindset

When we begin our careers, we are typically in a beginner's mindset. We are excited about the possibilities that we see available. We set high-achievement goals and strive to be the best version of ourselves. But at some point, we may find ourselves burnt out, tired and just sick of the system. Our balloon has been burst by microaggressions, bias, discrimination, and exclusion.

The growth mindset is then replaced with a fixed mindset. Adapting to a fixed mindset is a place that you do not want to remain. This mindset makes you believe all the things people have said about you or to you. Have you had any of these things said to you: "You'll never be more than (insert your role/title)." "Why would you want to pursue that?" "People like you generally stay in this field, stay here and you'll do well." "Minorities usually don't do well in this area; you can make more of a difference staying here managing other minorities and being a role model for them."

After hearing these types of comments over time, it can be a major blow to your confidence. You may even begin to believe some of these comments and your mindset shifts from growing to being fixed and complacent. You may even become bitter and resentful and feel stuck.

One of my close friends experienced this in her career. She worked in finance and was managing a diverse team of individuals who didn't respect her because she was a woman and, to top it off, a black woman. She sought advice and guidance from her leader and other peers only to be told to "grow a thick skin" and do more to win them over.

She went above and beyond and even overboard to win them over, only to feel more disrespected as time went on. One day we met for lunch, and I asked her one very important question: Whose definition of success was she striving for? She thought for a moment and replied she was going after her definition of success because she was working at a prestigious firm, had a management role, high paying salary etc. I then asked her who was winning... herself or the company?

She paused and after a few moments whispered they were winning, and she didn't even realize it. Hello!! We then went on to discuss how in fact she was not following her goals and aspirations and how she had become so fixated on proving them wrong and letting everyone see that she could be all things to everyone and solve everything herself she had lost herself. This experience is very relatable and if you change a few details, we all have probably been in her shoes in some shape or form.

How To Do It?

To keep operating in a growth mindset, at all times, we must know ourselves.

What are your values, beliefs, and principles; reflect thoughtfully and then write them down in your brag book and keep them close to you. Identify your purpose and see how you can move beyond your comfort zone.

These steps will then help you to see how you can create the environment that will help you thrive and help you to continue winning!

Take time to review your mindset and identify what space you are operating in. Transforming your thoughts enables you to change your behavior and improve your performance, thus increasing your confidence. The clarity that comes from operating in a growth mindset empowers you to make time and space for the opportunities that serve you. You will no longer hold on to something that is no longer serving you.

Let it go! When you let go of things that no longer serve you, you allow space for new opportunities to flow in. You are free to aspire to what you want and achieve YOUR success!

PAUSE, THINK & ASK: (P.T.A.)

The next time you feel like you're stuck or in a negative mindset, **Pause, Think, and Ask Yourself:**

☐ What barriers are currently blocking me?

☐ Who or what can I tap into to assist me in changing my perspective and outlook?

☐ Would a change of environment allow me to operate in a more positive mindset?

If the answers to those questions make you feel confident and secure, then proceed. If they don't, begin identifying and removing the barriers that are hindering you from operating in a growth mindset!

Pause.

Think...

Ask!

(TAKE SOME TIME AND REFLECT)

"Don't wait around for other people to be happy for you. Any happiness you get you've got to make yourself."

– ALICE WALKER

Clear
Tip. 9 *Out*
Your Closet

Spring cleaning is a good time to clear out any clutter and get rid of or pack away things you are no longer using. How do you feel after cleaning out your closet? I feel great because I now have made room for new shoes, bags, and clothes.

The spring cleaning that we are going to discuss now has to do with cleaning out your mind of any limiting beliefs that have settled there and taken up space. It is time to let go of any thoughts and ideas that tear down your confidence. What do you need to declutter to begin this process? It may be relationships that you are holding onto that no longer serve your purpose.

Some people come into our lives for a season, a reason, or a lifetime. Whose season and /or reason has expired? Is your job cluttering up your life? Have you allowed yourself to remain in a position or with a company that is tearing you down rather than building you up? If you are an entrepreneur, are you holding onto a business that you need to let go of, but you are fearful of being seen as a failure?

Do you have family members that constantly drain you; personally, and financially? Have you allowed self-care to become non-existent and sacrificed it to work those extra hours or do something for a friend/family member that you should have declined? Remember your boundaries.

How To Do It?

As you look at your "closet," what things have you outgrown that you need to get rid of? It could be too small, too big or worn out. Pack it up and send it to the "landfill."

No one goes to the landfill to retrieve their trash, once it lands there it is gone forever. Identify what things you are going to send to the landfill.

Make a list and put dates next to each item that will be discarded. It's time to make room for the new!

Now that you have cleaned and decluttered, you have room for clarity. You can begin to understand yourself even better and spend time doing self-care and self-development. When you have clarity, you can make smarter and wiser decisions.

There is more room for confidence to flourish because your limiting beliefs have been diminished and the blockers and barriers have been disposed of.

This step may be extremely difficult if you have not decluttered in years or even thought about spring cleaning. This will be a mindset shift for you, but one that is extremely important to your growth.

Revisit your purpose and your vision, and review what blockers or challenges are standing in the way of your success. Those are the things that need to be cleaned out!

There may be an individual at work that is a thorn in your flesh. It could be your leader, peer, or direct report. This person has been taking up space in your closet. You dread any interaction you must have with them; you avoid having to speak to them in meetings or constantly think about how you can reduce the amount of time you have to spend working on projects with them. They are causing you stress and anxiety. How will you begin the declutter process?

Revisit your boundaries and limit your interaction with them.

You have the power to say no to collaborating with this person if they are causing you distress and affecting your mental health. If the situation does not improve, ask yourself: what am I sacrificing?

How is this situation serving my purpose? If it does not, then it's time to declutter and make some changes. Growing your confidence includes knowing when it's ok to say "no" and sticking to that decision. Strategic thinking can guide you in how to manage the situation tactfully and professionally. It may involve speaking with your leader about moving this person to another department or perhaps removing yourself from the situation.

Pull out your calendar right now and schedule your spring cleaning, it's one of the best decisions you can make for yourself. Make space for yourself and what serves you, it's the best feeling to feel free, clean, and in control.

PAUSE, THINK &
ASK: (P.T.A.)

The next time you feel overwhelmed or burnt out,
Pause, Think, and Ask Yourself:

☐ What have I allowed to creep into my life that is causing burnout?

☐ Am I respecting and adhering to my boundaries?

☐ How many times have I practiced self-care in the last month?

If the answers to those questions make you feel confident and secure, then proceed. If they don't, stop right now and decide on one action that you can incorporate immediately to begin cleaning out your closet!

Pause.

Think...

Ask!

(TAKE SOME TIME AND REFLECT)

"If people are doubting how far you can go, go so far that you can't hear them anymore."

– MICHELE RUIZ

Celebrate Your *Tip. 10* Wins

When a team wins a championship game or achieves a huge goal, they celebrate.

Our confidence grows every time we have a win, no matter how big or small. It is time to normalize celebrating your wins! Have you ever felt proud of yourself for doing something that meant the world to you, only to have a co-worker or manager diminish its importance? I remember working on an exceedingly difficult coding project, a project that included incorporating many new aspects of the business and then producing a report for the leadership team.

I admit I sacrificed much time and energy to complete this project and did not set the boundaries I should have. When the project was finally completed, I felt excellent! It stretched me and increased my knowledge and skill set. However, my manager responded in a way that made me feel like it was something that I should have done, and it was nothing special. I had to take off some personal days to recover and rebuild my confidence. I did an amazing job and the impact this project had on the business was tremendous.

This experience taught me to never let anyone else diminish my worth and contributions. If it means something to you, then it is important and should be celebrated. Recall that time someone at work took credit for your work or did not acknowledge you for your contribution.

I can feel my blood pressure rising as I begin to think back to occasions when I allowed this to happen early in my career. I became conditioned to accept that was how things were. I would do my work and keep my head down. After all, I told myself, "You should be thankful to have this job and be in this position." I had adopted a fixed mindset.

Yes, I did say that I allowed myself to be put in these situations.

While I cannot control the actions of others, I can control how I respond to situations.

I learned that when I am working on something to speak up, involve others, let them know how the work that I am doing is progressing. Do not work with your head down in silence, others will take your work and celebrate in public.

Realize that sometimes you are placed in situations that will not allow you to win.

No matter what you do, you will not be successful in that situation. When you realize that, move, act, and think differently. Step back and strategically think about what success looks like for that project or task. Is it something that you can accomplish and still stick to your boundaries?

Is it serving your purpose and providing the impact that you wish to provide? And even if it does not turn out the way you envision it, can you be proud of the effort and time that you put into it? If it does, it is worth celebrating!

Another factor that is incorporated into your mindset, from an early age, is to be humble and not brag. Let your work speak for itself. That's fine, but closed mouths don't get raises, promotions, or bonuses! I'm not advising you to "pat yourself on the back" on every occasion in front of everyone. We have all worked or been in the company of someone who constantly brags about how important they are and everything that they have accomplished.

Nobody wants to be around that person! But use your intuition and identify the appropriate occasions to "congratulate yourself," because if you don't then who will?

How To Do It?

Identify one occasion in the upcoming weeks where you can showcase your impact, it may be in a 1-on-1 meeting with your leader or in a team meeting. Showcase your swag!

Internal and external celebrations are huge confidence boosters. After completing a project or getting a win, doing your happy dance in your office behind closed doors can feel amazing. But can you imagine how it would feel if you went into the hallway outside your office/cubicle and did that happy celebratory dance. You will smile from ear to ear and I bet others will join you as well.

Have you been eyeing that pair of shoes or that bag that would look stunning on your arm? Or maybe you have been wanting to try that new restaurant or get that new book by your favorite author?

It could be something as simple and satisfying as sitting on your porch and drinking a cup of tea or making yourself a bubble bath. Whatever things you may have been wanting to do or saving for a special day or occasion, today is the day, celebrate yourself and go do it!

Your Brag book, vision board and Values and Beliefs list are also all instrumental in celebrating your wins. These are made by you and for you.

Use them to celebrate your accomplishments often and always. Never let anyone diminish your light, no one lights a candle and sits it under a basket.

Let your light shine for the world to see and your authentic confidence will shine brightly!

PAUSE, THINK &
ASK: (P.T.A.)

The next time you do something amazing or accomplish a goal, **Pause, Think, and Ask Yourself:**

☐ What can I do to celebrate myself at this moment?

☐ If my best friend accomplished what I just did, how would I celebrate them? Do this for yourself!

☐ Am I dimming my light to allow others to shine?

If the answers to those questions make you feel confident and secure, then proceed. If they don't, then go celebrate one of your accomplishments, do not put it off!

Pause.

Think...

Ask!

(TAKE SOME TIME AND REFLECT)

"Think like a queen. A queen is not afraid to fail. Failure is another stepping stone to greatness."

– Oprah Winfrey

Conclu-
sion.

Stepping into your authentic confidence is a journey. It is something that we will continue to master as long as we live. You will constantly learn more about yourself and what makes you special.

Embrace this and never apologize for being you. Show up as your genuine authentic confident self on every occasion that you can.

I have never been ashamed of the beautiful skin color that God gave me. Yes, at times I have been made to feel less because of the color of my skin and I have allowed those occasions to diminish my confidence and shrink back into the shadows.

I have allowed others to dictate my career aspirations and put a stop sign where there should be a big green "go" sign.

Those experiences have enhanced my appreciation for who I am and my unique gifts. I can now help other WOC to navigate the corporate environment and feel confident in their own skin.

YOU ARE

Beautiful.

Smart.

Genuine.

Authentic.

You Are Confident!

Acknowled-gements

Writing this book has always been something that I wanted to do but lacked the confidence. Well, look at me now, authentic confidence in action! I had so much support to make this dream a reality and I could not have done it without the support of my village.

To all my family, friends, colleagues, mentors, coaches, and teachers, thank you for pushing me to always be the best, and to continue to challenge myself because you saw greatness in me even when I couldn't see it in myself.

About *Hayley*

Hayley Dennis is an executive, leadership and career coach, master facilitator, author, speaker, and wife.

Her mission is to teach women of color how to build authentic confidence and navigate the corporate world with purpose and vision. She began her career in Corporate America at the age of 16 and has expanded her knowledge and training tremendously by working in several different industries.

She applies her vast professional experiences, reliable knowledge, and practical lessons to assist women in recognizing and reaching their full potential both professionally and personally.

About
The Authentic
Confidence
Lounge

The Authentic Confidence Lounge is a community where WOC feel supported, confident and realize that you are not the only one feeling this way.

A place where you can build authentic confidence and not feel like a fraud. You do not have to compare yourselves to others. Step into your confidence and be a bold confident woman who isn't afraid of success and accomplishment.

Learn more about Hayley and come join her in the Authentic Confidence Lounge at:

authenticconfidencelounge.com

Sign-up Now!